THE FOUR **HANDS**

Requirements for Rebuilding Your Destiny

Festus Adeyeye

THE FOUR HANDS

[Requirements for Rebuilding Your Destiny]

ISBN 13: 978-1-7343991-1-0

EDITED BY: Titilola A. Akinyemi

PUBLISHED BY: Platform for Success Press

+1 917 826 3566, press@platformforsuccess.org

ORDERING INFORMATION:

To order books and tapes by Festus Adeyeye, please write to:

Festus Adeyeye
Adeyeye Evangelistic Ministries (AEM)
P.O. Box 810,
West Hempstead, NY 11552
E-mail: adevministries@gmail.com

TABLE OF CONTENTS

INTRODUCTION

"Therefore whoever hears these sayings of Mine, and does them, I will liken him to a wise man who built his house on the rock: and the rain descended, the floods came, and the winds blew and beat on that house; and it did not fall, for it was founded on the rock. "But everyone who hears these sayings of Mine, and does not do them, will be like a foolish man who built his house on the sand: and the rain descended, the floods came, and the winds blew and beat on that house; and it fell. And great was its fall" [Matthew 7:24-26 (NKJV)].

Life is more of a journey than a destination. In the journey of life, we are all engaged in the building and rebuilding of our destinies, families, communities and nations. From Jesus Christ's words above, the adventure of life is like a building project, where professionals utilize raw materials to construct different kinds of buildings; buildings that range from hamlets, to bungalows, magnificent palaces, and eye-catching modern-day edifices. And just like in building construction, the task of building or rebuilding destinies also requires a degree of planning, preparation, precision, pursuit and perseverance.

There are four hands usually present in any destiny rebuilding project. Three of them are good and desirable, while the fourth is undesirable, but rears its head, uninvited, most of the time. It is almost impossible to succeed in the kingdom without adequate knowledge of these four hands and the ability to apply the three good hands, while carefully addressing all four. That is, success in the kingdom is maximizing the desirable hands and halting the operations of the undesirable one.

My questions to you this moment are;

- Where are you in life, and what are you building?
- Have you progressed in certain areas of your life and desire to achieve more?
- Are you experiencing difficulties at this moment while making the effort to rebuild all or certain areas of your life?
- Are there areas of your life that have broken down or areas in which you have suffered setbacks and you seek to rebuild?

Rest assured that rebuilding for a comeback is possible. You can overcome all setbacks and experience a complete turnaround. Irrespective of where you are at this moment, maximizing the operations of these hands will enhance your ability to make adequate and sustainable progress. There are unfailing principles that will grant you stress-less victory when diligently applied.

Life always has two sides. If you are poor, it is only a side of life and not the end. If you are due for marriage and are still single, it is just one side of life and not the end. If you are given a medical report of a terminal illness with seemingly no hope, it is just one side of life and not a finality. You must never concede defeat and conclude on your destiny while on the bad side of life, as there is another side that can lead you to victory. People are overwhelmed, discouraged, and heartbroken about life, when they focus only on its bad side. There is a better and more glorious life, and you have been equipped with what it takes to make sustainable progress.

1

DOWN, BUT NOT DONE

"Rejoice not against me, O mine enemy: when I fall, I shall arise; when I sit in darkness, the Lord shall be a light unto me" (Micah 7:8).

That you are down, does not mean that you are done. There is life beyond the storm. There is meaningful life after you have suffered defeat in any area of your life; be it a divorce, the loss of a loved one, the loss of a job, a major financial setback, or bankruptcy, etc. Everyone in life must learn to build a meaningful destiny from scratch or learn to rebuild even after suffering the loss of anything in life. Nehemiah exemplified how to rebuild broken dreams in the midst of very fierce opposition. He demonstrated how one can become successful in spite of the obstacles of life. The life of Nehemiah shows how one can build a successful career, successful organization, and successful life, in the midst of seemingly overwhelming opposition.

The book of Nehemiah is a book of courage, wisdom, and grace in starting and finishing any project or divine assignment. In the days of Nehemiah, the walls of cities were symbols of security and pride. The wall then, was a defense to prevent external invaders from entering the city. Whenever the wall of a city is broken, it lacks security and is susceptible to attacks from invaders. In the time of Nehemiah, the Babylonian empire fought the Israelites, devastated their cities and took most of them captives into exile. This left the cities in ruins for many years including the walls. After they were released from captivity, some chose to remain in exile while some came back. Most of them were so discouraged and indifferent to any effort in rebuilding their cities or their own personal lives. No matter what has broken down in your life, never allow discouragement or the spirit of indifference and insignificance to control you. Discouragement is a thief; a robber of destiny.

When trying to forge ahead in life, there are times we experience oppositions and rejections. There are times that we experience partial or total breakdown. Ask yourself therefore; "What part of your life is broken that looks irreparable?" "Where has life dealt you a blow and you are wondering how to move ahead?" This material aims to lift your spirit and challenge you to rebuild and bounce back. You may be down, but you are not done with life. You may be down, but you are not done winning. You may be down, but you are not done rising. Despite oppositions and challenges that were meant to discourage and stop him, Nehemiah completed the rebuilding of the broken walls of Jerusalem in a record 52 days. There are several principles you can learn from

Nehemiah that will help you to succeed in your undertakings. These are principles that you can leverage that will help you to rebuild your dreams, your marriage, your career, your health and your destiny in totality. Even if you have no idea on how to start life in general, this book will give you some insight on how to. It will give you some insight on how to lay the proper foundation on building life in general, and enhance your journey for a flourishing finishing.

The adventure of life is similar to a building project; as such, we need to approach every area of our lives like a building project. Whether starting and running a successful marriage, raising children, starting and running a ministry, starting and running a successful business or relationships, we must know that it is like a building project. Many elements are necessary for starting and finishing a building project, and the same concept obtains, when building meaningful aspects of life. There are coordinated attempts, planning, and forces necessary for success in any area of life. Good and great things do not just happen in life. There is no marriage, business, ministry, family, etc. that become successful just by themselves, without proper coordinated endeavors and actions. The success or failure of any endeavor is related to the approach and attitude of those involved.

God has ordained for you and me to build a successful marriage, successful enterprises, and successful and impactful destinies, but not without adequately coordinated efforts on our part.

"For which of you, intending to build a tower, does not sit down first and count the cost, whether he has enough to finish

it — lest, after he has laid the foundation, and is not able to fin-
ish, all who see it begin to mock him" (Luke 14:28-29).

From the words of Jesus Christ in this scripture, destiny building should not be approached casually, but with intentional planning. You are where you are now because of your past choices, actions, and decision. If you do not like your life in its current state, you can choose to make decisions and choices that will transform your destiny. You can start to rebuild, despite present and obvious challenges.

2

LIFE-REBUILDING LESSONS
FROM NEHEMIAH

The lessons from the book of Nehemiah on the rebuilding of the broken walls of Jerusalem, are so relevant in any rebuilding effort. They give a clear understanding of how to prepare, plan, pursue, persevere and finish our intended work. Nehemiah was a visionary leader with the ability to see a problem, identify strategic solutions, and rally others to implement the strategies, under several circumstances. His name Nehemiah, means "the Lord's comfort," and his visionary struggles brought comfort to God's people in a time of great need. As kingdom people, we must have Nehemiah's mindset. Although he was comfortable as the king's cup bearer, he ventured out of his comfort zone in order to bring comfort to his nation by rebuilding the walls of Jerusalem.

Progress in life is neither the absence of problems, nor absence of failures; but rather, the ability to put broken pieces back together.

It is developing strategies, grit and the forthrightness to forge ahead. There are certain steps required to rebuild every broken part of our lives. Is there something broken in your life that you would like to fix, but do not know how? A broken marriage? A failing business? A dying relationship? Or, is there something that has fallen apart that you would like to rebuild? A house? A church? A ministry? A career? If so, then you will appreciate the lessons in rebuilding, that can be found in the biblical book of Nehemiah.

Nehemiah took on a rebuilding project that seemed imposing, impractical, and nearly impossible. However, when he told God what he wanted to do, God gave him the green light to do it, and walked him through every step of the project. With God's help, Nehemiah and his people rebuilt a wall around the entire city of Jerusalem.

People told Nehemiah it was impossible; people tried to stop his work; people threatened his life; but Nehemiah pressed on. After many months of planning, praying, fighting and building, the work was finally complete. The surrounding countries - including his enemies - saw what Nehemiah had done, and they also knew *how* he accomplished it. The book of Nehemiah says,

> *"...they realized that this work had been done with the help of our God" (Nehemiah 6:16).*

IDENTIFY YOUR BUILDING PROJECT

We can see from Nehemiah's model, that foundational step for any successful rebuilding effort is to identify what is to be built, and to have a vision for the project goals. This is because rebuilding is almost impossible until you can visualize it. It takes seeing and acknowledging a problem to proffer solutions to fixing the problem. You must therefore have a strong desire for a rebuilding project, in order to build or rebuild any meaningful area of your life. Until you acknowledge that there is a problem, you cannot solve it. Until you acknowledge the need for a new direction, you cannot make any effort towards that direction. There is the need to have the understanding that you ought to step higher; that is, you must have a burden, for that particular area of your life.

Life does not give you what you deserve; it gives you what you desire and pursue. Whatever you do not desire cannot be delivered. And whatever you do not pursue cannot be produced. Nehemiah saw the broken walls, and he developed a burden and desire to rebuild. Nehemiah was not the only one who saw the broken walls. Many saw it but perceived it differently. It is not impossible that some did see it as a burden, but never developed the burden to the point of rebuilding. Nehemiah most likely saw it as a shame to the nation. He saw its rebuilding as a necessity to regaining the security and the pride of the city. He was so burdened by what he saw that he wept, mourned, and prayed (Nehemiah 1:4). The king also noticed his sad countenance (Nehemiah 2:2).

Next levels are always available but only if identified, desired, pursued, and captured.

> *"Therefore I say unto you, What things soever ye desire, when ye pray, believe that ye receive them, and ye shall have them"* *(Mark 11:24).*

The starting point and one of the keys to answered prayers, is desire.

> *"And Jabez called on the God of Israel saying, "Oh, that You would bless me indeed, and enlarge my territory, that Your hand would be with me, and that You would keep me from evil, that I may not cause pain!" So God granted him what he requested"* *[1 Chronicles 4:10 (NKJV)].*

Jabez had a burden and a desire never to be a source of pain, since his name meant "because he was born in pain." So by birth, pain was to be permanently attached to his destiny. He, however, called on God to bless him and break the curse of shame. And out of such burden and desire, he prayed to God for a change. God granted his request, and Jabez became more honorable than his brethren.

ASSESS YOUR BUILDING REQUIREMENTS

The next step is to conduct an initial assessment of your building project requirements. Nehemiah did this by evaluating the broken walls of the city. The assessments can be summed up by answering the pertinent questions of "what," "why," and "how."

1. What are the problems? What is it that is broken and needs fixing?
2. Why did the problem manifest?
3. How do I go about fixing the problem?

"So I came to Jerusalem and was there three days. Then I arose in the night, I and a few men with me; I told no one what my God had put in my heart to do at Jerusalem; nor was there any animal with me, except the one on which I rode. And I went out by night through the Valley Gate to the Serpent Well and the Refuse Gate, and viewed the walls of Jerusalem which were broken down and its gates which were burned with fire. Then I went on to the Fountain Gate and to the King's Pool, but there was no room for the animal under me to pass. So I went up in the night by the valley, and viewed the wall; then I turned back and entered by the Valley Gate, and so returned" (Nehemiah 2:11-15).

Assessment is very important for adequate preparation. Knowing the extent of the damage helps to determine what you need, who you need and how long it will take to rectify the problem. Many people rush into things they are not prepared to handle and eventually stop short of finishing.

EVALUATE AND GATHER YOUR RESOURCES

No matter how great or clear a vision is, provisions are essential to its fulfilment. It may be resources of people, money, or other necessary things. The questions to be answered are;

1. What resources do I have at hand now relative to my intended goal?
2. What resources can I obtain from my region of influence?
3. How can I obtain the necessary resources?

Nehemiah prayed for favor and approached the king for the necessary resources. He asked the king to give him time-off to do the job. He sought the favor of the king to give him a letter to secure timbers from the keeper of timber, etc.

SUMMARY OF REQUIREMENTS

Jesus said in the book of Luke;

> *"Suppose one of you wants to build a tower. Won't you first sit down and estimate the cost to see if you have enough money to complete it? For if you lay the foundation and are not able to finish it, everyone who sees it will ridicule you, saying, 'This person began to build and wasn't able to finish'" (Luke 14:28-30).*

As taught by Jesus Christ in the scripture above, the steps to be considered before embarking on any venture can be summarized as follows:

1. Evaluate your current condition. What do I want to do? What do I need to change? What habits do I want to break? Where am I going? Develop a clear sense direction, since you cannot accomplish what you cannot outline.

2. Design your building project. This requires that you pro-actively pause to think and plan. Thinking is hard work, and it is usually easier to work with your hands than to work with your brain. It is also easier however, to work on a process that your brain has already mapped out.

3. Envision the end product.

4. Estimate the costs. What price am I going to pay? Am I ready to pay the price? What will this cost me in terms of the resources of time, money, skilled labor, etc.?

5. Commit to its completion. Stay on course, until your desired end is achieved. Avoid the pitfall of the fear of failing. There is no successful person that has never failed. They use failure as a tool, for their success.

3

THE FOUR HANDS

"Then said I unto them, Ye see the distress that we are in, how Jerusalem lieth waste, and the gates thereof are burned with fire: come, and let us build up the wall of Jerusalem, that we be no more a reproach. Then I told them of the hand of my God which was good upon me; as also the king's words that he had spoken unto me. And they said, Let us rise up and build. So they strengthened their hands for this good work. But when Sanballat the Horonite, and Tobiah the servant, the Ammonite, and Geshem the Arabian, heard it, they laughed us to scorn, and despised us, and said, What is this thing that ye do? will ye rebel against the king? Then answered I them, and said unto them, The God of heaven, he will prosper us; therefore we his servants will arise and build: but ye have no portion, nor right, nor memorial, in Jerusalem" (Nehemiah 2:17-20).

"So the wall was finished in the twenty and fifth day of the month Elul, in fifty and two days" (Nehemiah 6:15).

To build anything meaningful in life, there are four hands that you cannot ignore.

[1] THE HANDS OF GOD

In any building or rebuilding effort, the first necessary hand is the hand of God. Many are weary, tired, and frustrated, in their daily pursuit of a better life, because they are building without God's involvement.

"And they went out and preached everywhere, the Lord working with them and confirming the word through the accompanying signs" [Mark 16:20 (NKJV)].

Nothing works unless God is at work with you. Unless God is in alliance with you, it is possible to struggle, toil, and labor without any meaningful result. However, when God is the builder, your labor becomes fruitful.

"Except the Lord build the house, they labor in vain that build it" (Psalms 127:1-2).

The first thing Nehemiah did was to pray to God for his gracious hand upon his life.

WHAT IS THE HAND OF GOD?

For the purpose of the subject matter of this book:

- The hand of God is divine approval from God.
- The hand of God is his involvement in any project or endeavor
- The hand of God is the favor of God upon a person, place, or thing.

"The gracious hand of my God was upon me" (Nehemiah 1:8).

- The hand of God is the manifestations of the power, presence, and the person of God in a life, endeavor, or project.

WHY DO YOU NEED THE HAND OF GOD.

Human endeavors without God's involvement can lead to frustration. I have learned that whatever is born out of God's approval will surely overcome obstacles and challenges of life.

"For whatsoever is born of God overcomes the world: and this is the victory that overcomes the world, even our faith" (1 John 5:4).

A ministry, marriage, business, or career that is born of God will always overcome any opposition. Therefore, meaningful and sustainable progress begins with God.

"And it came to pass, when I heard these words, that I sat down and wept, and mourned certain days, and fasted, and prayed before the God of heaven," (Nehemiah 1:4).

"I also told them about the gracious hand of my God on me and what the king had said to me. They replied, "Let us start rebuilding." So they began this good work" (Nehemiah 2:18).

Although Nehemiah was passionate about rebuilding the wall of Jerusalem, he did not make any move until he secured God's approval. Why?.

- Whenever you secure divine approval, you are guaranteed divine direction.
- Whenever you secure divine approval, you are guaranteed divine backing.
- Whenever you secure divine approval, you are guaranteed divine supplies and provision.
- Whenever you secure divine approval, you are guaranteed divine protection. When God's hands rest upon you, no force will be able to contend against your life.

"Trust in the Lord with all thine heart; and lean not unto thine own understanding. In all thy ways acknowledge him, and he shall direct thy paths" (Proverbs 3:5-6).

In 1 Samuel 30:1-9, David also rebuilt, and he experienced full restoration of lost family and properties, by seeking God's guidance first. He enquired of the Lord for direction on how to proceed.

Securing the hand of God; God's divine approval, can be done by seeking God through prayers and fasting, having intimate walks with God, and building a relationship with the Holy Spirit. When we seek God genuinely, we receive insight, directions, vision and instructions for our next levels.

[2] YOUR OWN HANDS

Irrespective of how many people are interested in helping you to rebuild your life, it will be absolutely impossible without your own active readiness and participation. There must be a readiness and the determination to give your destiny all it takes to succeed. After Nehemiah was done securing God's approval in Nehemiah 1, he commenced efforts to rebuild the wall from chapter 2 onwards. He set the goals, requested for a letter of protection and provision of resources such as timber for the rebuilding project (Nehemiah 2:6-8). When Nehemiah told them of the gracious hand of God upon him, the people did not go to sleep but rather went to work (Nehemiah 2:18). The people had the mind to work (Nehemiah 2:18; Nehemiah 4:6). Thank God for securing divine direction, for favored connections, and for the prophecies you have been given. However, you need to work as if your life depends on it. You cannot just wish for what you want or hope for what you want; you must have a plan and work on it. When God grants you approval in the arena of your divine assignment, you must back it up with visionary pursuit, skillful diligence, hard work and wise actions. You must be willing to go beyond where others have gone. An outcome is not extraordinary by itself; it is the extraordinary input of man that results in extraordinary outcomes.

In 1 Samuel 30, when David received the instruction to pursue, overtake and recover all that the enemy stole from him and from his men, he did not just wait for the manifestations. He assembled his willing men and pursued the enemies.

"Diligent hands will rule, but laziness ends in forced labor" *(Proverbs 12:24).*

Your ability to rule and reign in life is tied to the function of your hands. Your hands represent the wise development and application of your skills for maximum productivity. Someone once said that your hands should be your "best friend," because many things are tied to your hands. Your hands define your position in life. Your hands define your class in life. Your hands define your rating in life. Conversely, the slothful hands shall be subjugated. No matter his height, color, or race, the slothful person remains under. If you do not want to end up as rubbish, do not be sluggish. What you do with your hands is what your hands do with you.

Another aspect of engaging your own hands is diligence. Diligence is the ladder to dominion and rulership. It is a known fact that everybody has opportunities in life. Diligence will embrace and maximize opportunities, while slothfulness will waste or miss opportunities.

WHAT IS DILIGENCE?

The basic definition of diligence is hard work. It is releasing your energy into your work. Working hard is key to flying high. It is the cure to a hard life. Only hard workers will end up as highflyers in their field of endeavor. Another expression of diligence is to be a tireless worker. We saw that in Genesis 26, as Isaac worked tirelessly and diligently. He kept digging and digging until he got to Rehoboth. And after he arrived at Rehoboth, he kept digging until he got to Beersheba. An advance definition of diligence is to be a creative and innovative worker, working daily and identifying ways to improve your work. Jacob experienced 20 years of hard labor and by creativity in Genesis 30:27-31, he experienced an uncommon harvest.

If you are diligent, you will be distinguished.

> *"Do you see a man skillful in his work? He will stand before kings; he will not stand before obscure men" (Proverbs 22:29).*

You can always tell where a diligent person will end. Examples are David, Joseph and Daniel who were slaves or captives in a strange land, but through diligence were elevated to sit among the kings. What makes people in life is not the certificate they obtain in school, but their diligence and ability to commit to a life of excellence.

Diligence terminates slavery. People naturally admire good workers. In Genesis 39: 1-6, Potiphar made Joseph the boss in the family. Diligent people are ever eager to work. They do not reject any assignment. They do not choose what to do. *"Whatsoever your hands find to do; do it with all your might,"* is their motto (Ecclesiastes 9:10). Before you find what you like to do, you must do that which you find.

As God's children, we have the culture of diligence because our God, the father, is a worker. Jesus attested to the fact that God the father works. But Jesus replied, *"My Father is always working, and so am I" (John 5:17).* In Genesis 2:15, the first thing God gave Adam in the garden after creating him was work; he gave him the responsibility to dress and keep the garden. God's son was a worker as well. "I must work the work," Jesus said (John 5:17; John 9:4). Diligent people place themselves under compulsion. (John 4:31). He worked and forgot about food (John 4:34-36; Luke 2:49). Also, Jesus went around doing good (Acts 10:38). Jesus went from city to city. You cannot give expression to the grace of God upon your life, in one position. Jesus went to where people were working, to select his disciples. He was very deliberate in his choices. For example, he found Peter at his place of fishing. He went to the custom table to observe Matthew, the tax collector, then called him as a disciple. EVERYONE GOD CALLED, WAS CALLED IN THE PLACE OF WORK. Moses was called while he was working. Amos was called where he was working. Peter was called while he was working. Gideon was called while he was keeping his father's field. Other examples of biblical references to finding work to do can be found in 1 Thessalonians 4:11, 2 Thessalonians 3:8-9, and Ephesians 4:28. And so, while grace and faith compliment work, they are in no way substitutes for work (1 Corinthians 15:10).

[3] THE HANDS OF OTHERS

The hands of others are necessary for your purposeful project completion. If you are going to build anything meaningful in life; be it a business, a company, a ministry, etc., you are going to need help from other people. One of the laws of success is that success travels on the bridge of relationships. While you may be able to create success on your own, traveling the journey of success with others makes it less stressful, more enjoyable and more rewarding. Everything God gives to you will be through human channels. God uses the hands of others to open doors. These human channels will be people that God has strategically positioned, touched and prepared to facilitate your destiny. They are known as destiny helpers.

Destiny helpers are those who use their resources and positions to advance your destiny. David's dream to recover all that the enemy stole from him was possible because of a man left behind by his master (1 Samuel 30:11). In order for the Israelites to conquer Jericho, they needed the help of Rahab the harlot. God uses the hands of others to open doors. Nehemiah sought favor to receive help for protection and timber. He also solicited helpers to build with him. We must be very skillful at building necessary relationships at each level of life. We must engage in cultivating strategic relationships, and team building. Always pray for the right people to come into your life. If God could use a harlot, he can use anybody, including unbelievers, to facilitate your destiny.

Behind every successful Steve Jobs is a Steve Wozniak, and there is a Paul Allen behind every successful Bill Gates. You need to have people that will help you achieve your dreams. You need mentors, partners, and so on. Some of the criteria for finding good partners and mentors are compatibility, experience, similar values, loyalty, and mutual benefit among many others. Even in the jail, Joseph had meaningful and valuable relationships with the Baker and the Butler. A dreamer walks with fellow dreamers, who may be millionaires in the making.

There are two kinds of people that can come into your life; a destiny enhancer or a destiny destroyer. Agents of increase or agents of decrease. Those who add value into your life or those who subtract value from your life.

> *"For what you had before I came was little, and it has increased to a great amount; the LORD has blessed you since my coming. And now, when shall I also provide for my own house?" [Genesis 30:30 (NKJV)].*

Jacob testified on how his presence in the house of Laban contributed positively to the life of Laban. Jacob served in the house of Laban for 20 years. The scripture above connotes seven messages to Laban from Jacob.

1. That what Laban had was little before Jacob came. That is, Laban was struggling prior to the arrival of Jacob.
2. That after Jacob's arrival, the little that Laban had increased.

3. That the Lord had blessed Laban for Jacob's sake. This was also confirmed by Laban in Genesis 30:27, where Laban said to Jacob,

   "Let me say this; I have learned by divination that the Lord has blessed me because of you."

4. That Jacob brought something to Laban's life that led to Laban's turnaround.
5. That Jacob's coming added value and profit to Laban's life.
6. That Jacob was Laban's destiny helper.
7. That Jacob's star lighted Laban's star and only then did Laban's star shine.

As founding Pastors of Abundant Life Christian Center Ministries, we appreciate the enormous contributions of other people in building the ministry from 7 adults in a living room to a mega church. It is obvious that my wife and I could not have done it alone. It was as a result of the efforts of several dedicated people with different talents. Geese are birds that are able to travel 71% further together than when traveling alone. You need a team because it is biblical, and it is effective. In no part of scripture do you have people working by themselves long term without the support of others. David had a band of men with him. Moses had Joshua, Aaron, Hur, Miriam, Bezalel and Oholiab, etc. Paul had a traveling team of 8 people. Jesus had a team of 12 men.

Nehemiah was able to build the wall of the city of Jerusalem because of teamwork. Half of the team worked while half were on guard, as a wall, four feet thick and twenty feet high was built, for the length of almost 1 mile. There are 28 instances of "next unto" and "after him" in the third chapter of the book of Nehemiah, indicating the different teams that contributed to the rebuilding of the walls. The key to success in building is thus building as a team. Everybody that aspires to be successful or build anything successful must build a team.

There are God-ordained relationships that God brings into our lives. We must learn how to discern, value, develop and maximize our God ordained connections. Take the story of Ruth and Naomi for example, as seen in Ruth 1:16 and similarly the story of Jesus and His disciples in John 6:65-69.

> *"And he said, Therefore, said I unto you, that no man can come unto me, except it were given unto him of my Father. From that time many of his disciples went back, and walked no more with him. Then said Jesus unto the twelve, Will ye also go away? Then Simon Peter answered him, Lord, to whom shall we go? thou hast the words of eternal life. And we believe and are sure that thou art that Christ, the Son of the living God."*

One of the ways to build an effective team is through networking. Statistics confirm that people prefer to do business with people they know, respect and trust. Businesses and careers are built on relationships. The more time you spend to build a network of clients, advisers, friends, and fans, the more successful you become. Networking is establishing contacts with necessary people with the sole aim of advancing a cause. Another word for it is team building. Effective networking, therefore, is all about developing relationships. In developing your own network, your job is to seek out those who know what you do not and who can help you connect where you cannot.

NURTURE YOUR GOD-ORDAINED CONNECTIONS.

1. Pray very well and be led by the Holy Spirit before you enter into any relationship.
2. Specifically ask God to send His ordained relationships into your life. Also, pray that God should give you the grace not to cultivate wrong (toxic) relationships. If you are already in one, be bold to terminate it.
3. The fact that somebody is very nice to you does not qualify him/her to be intimately involved in your life.
4. Finally, do not burn bridges in relationships. Always check yourself and be careful to exhibit godly character that will allow you to maintain relationships. Some relationships are meant to be maintained, while some should be distant. Some, you need to nurture, and some, you need to sever.

**HOW TO IDENTIFY HEALTHY INFLUENCERS
AND DESTINY HELPERS**

Everyone you come into contact with will fall into one of four categories:

"SUBSTRACTORS," "MULTIPLIERS," "DIVIDERS," and "ADDERS."

Some relationships should be avoided because they sap away your life and blur your focus. Be friendly and courteous to everyone, but be selective about who influences you.

To determine who will be allowed into your space to the extent of being an influence on you, you must learn two skills:

1. The art of creating limited association. There are some people that you cannot completely avoid; but you can control the influence they have in your life. How? By controlling the amount of time, you spend with them.

2. The art of creating expanded association. Identify the people who add value to your life, and arrange your schedule, so you can spend more time with them. Even a small amount of time with the right people can make a great deal of difference.

To classify people by these two associations, you must ask yourself;

- **Who am I spending my time with?** What kind of people are they? What are their goals, their values, their world views and their attitude to life?

- **What are their roles in my life?** It is your responsibility to discern the role that each person is assigned to play in your life. Some are sent to mentor you; as such, do not try to make them your Buddy- buddy. An example would be your spiritual mentors. Some are assigned to be your friend; do not make them your mentors. Some are even sent to be mentored by you; again, do not make them your own mentor. Someone may qualify to mentor you in your career, but not in your spiritual life. Your Certified Public Accountant (CPA) who guides you in your financial matters should not be designated to mentor you on your marriage. Do not confuse the roles people are assigned to play in your life.

- **What effect do they have on me?** Where do they have me going? How have they got me thinking or talking? What have they got me reading or watching or doing? What has become acceptable or unacceptable since this relationship began? How are they affecting my growth, my performance, my productivity, and my creativity? What am I becoming as a result of this connection?

- **Are all answers acceptable to me?** If your response to this last question is "No," then you must do something about that connection. Some connections you will sever, while you will redefine others.

Jesus had a relationship with the crowds that was different from his relationship with the seventy. He had a more intimate relationship with the twelve, than he did with the seventy (Luke 10:1; Mark 3:14-19). Among the twelve, Jesus had a measure of relationship with the three (Peter, James, and John), that he did not have with other nine. There are places that Jesus took the three that he did not take the other nine. He also had an intimate relationship with John the beloved, that he did not have with the rest.

HOW DO YOU DECIDE WHO QUALIFIES?

1. People who are absolutely committed to God's word. People who have an unapologetic commitment to a biblical worldview. Their choices, their behaviors, their values, and their lifestyles are governed by scripture. People who do not only claim to be Christians, but show the practical fruit as evidence.
2. People who bring out the best in you.
3. People who improve and empower you. They are called adders and multipliers. These are the people who are not intimidated by your success and progress.
4. People who are so committed to your ultimate success that they are not afraid to tell you when you get it wrong or commend and rejoice with you when you make progress. However, be very careful that you do not surround yourself with those who sing your praises only, or those who consistently berate you. They must be people who genuinely love and care for you.
5. People who are going in the direction that you are going. They may be ahead of you or behind you, but they are moving in the same direction.

Remember that when God wants to bless you, he sends someone into your life. Elisha had Elijah. Ruth had a Naomi. Pharaoh had a Joseph. Joseph had a butler. The Ethiopian Eunuch had a Philip. The Philippian jailor had a Paul. Paul had a Barnabas. Timothy had Eunice and Paul.

You have a "SOMEBODY"... and somebody has YOU!!!

The way you treat your God-ordained connections will determine whether or not your relationships with them are long-term.

[4] THE UNWANTED HANDS OF OPPOSITION

"Be sober, be vigilant; because your adversary the devil, as a roaring lion, walks about, seeking whom he may devour:" (1 Peter 5:8).

Without fear, Satan has been identified as an adversary who contends against any meaningful step you take in advancing your destiny. He uses different schemes and methods. Sometimes, he uses people within or outside to weary your hands, to intimidate you, and even to viciously attack you. Therefore, whenever you make up your mind to build your life, opposition may arise. Sanballat and Tobiah ridiculed, slandered and try severally to discourage Nehemiah and his men during the rebuilding of the broken walls of Jerusalem.

"But it came to pass, that when Sanballat heard that we builded the wall, he was wroth, and took great indignation, and mocked the Jews. And he spake before his brethren and the army of Samaria, and said, What do these feeble Jews? will they fortify themselves? will they sacrifice? will they make an end in a day? will they revive the stones out of the heaps of the rubbish which are burned? Now Tobiah the Ammonite was by him, and he said, Even that which they build, if a fox go up, he shall even break down their stone wall" (Nehemiah 4:1-3).

"But when Sanballat the Horonite, and Tobiah the servant, the Ammonite, and Geshem the Arabian, heard it, they laughed us to scorn, and despised us, and said, What is this thing that ye do? will ye rebel against the king? Then answered I them, and said unto them, The God of heaven, he will prosper us; therefore we his servants will arise and build: but ye have no portion, nor right, nor memorial, in Jerusalem" (Nehemiah 2:19-20).

Also in Genesis 26:20-21, the Philistines resisted Isaac's attempts to dig wells for procuring water, crucial to his flourishing as a farmer with his flocks. Every time Isaac and his men dug a well, the Philistines closed it, but Isaac refused to allow their contention and hatred stop him. He kept digging after every aggression by the enemy, until he finally got to Rehoboth; which was his place of roominess; a place of victory.

To successfully build in life, your determination to accomplish your goals and fulfill your destiny must be stronger than the enemies' resolve to stop you. Despite the opposition, Nehemiah and his men, prayed, plan, engaged in strategic work and posted a watch in order to overcome the plot of the enemy. Instead of allowing yourself to be distracted, stay focused on your rebuilding plan (Nehemiah 4:14-17). Nehemiah succeeded through prayer, consistent effort, refusal to be intimidated, trusting God and remaining focused on the plan.

THE SIX TYPES OF OPPOSITION

Nehemiah experienced six types of opposition which are typical of what everyone may experience in the attempt to build or rebuild his or her destiny. It is therefore necessary to have a biblical plan of dealing with the following oppositions.

1. THE ANGER OF OTHERS AGAINST YOU

Whenever you rise up to rebuild your life and destiny, expect anger from some people. Their focus is to stop you from your intended goals. There are people or systems that for them, your excellence reveals their mediocrity and thus, they will come against you. Sanballat, the governor of Samaria, became furious and very angry (Nehemiah 4:1,7). The Hebrew word for furious and angry means "burning mad." Sanballat was the governor of Samaria and he knew that a secured, well-fortified and independent Jerusalem would threaten his hold on the area, and undermine his control of the trade route through the region, thus hurting his economy. So for a period of time, he dropped his differences with the Ammonites to the East, the Arabs to the South, and the Philistines to the West. In anger over what Nehemiah was doing they all came together, threatening to stop the work by violence, if necessary.

2. MOCKERY AND SARCASM

Sanballat and his evil allies gathered within hearing distance of the wall and asked sarcastic questions.

"And in the presence of his associates and the army of Samaria, he said, "What are those feeble Jews doing? Will they restore their wall? Will they offer sacrifices? Will they finish in a day? Can they bring the stones back to life from those heaps of rubble – burned as they are?" 3 Tobiah the Ammonite, who was at his side, said, "What they are building – even a fox climbing up on it would break down their wall of stones!" (Nehemiah 4:2-3).

Mockery and sarcasm is with the intent of belittling your efforts, so you can have a feeling of worthlessness and insignificance. Satan can use your thoughts or speak through men to disparage you, with the intent to weary and weaken your resolve. So, in your attempt to build or rebuild your destiny, watch out for ridicule and mockery. As they say today, "it comes with the territory." You must know that it is simply an effort to stifle the progress of your project.

3. THREATS AND INTIMIDATION.

If anger and ridicule do not work, the enemy becomes more aggressive. They may use threats of violence (Nehemiah 4:8, 11). Satan still uses subtle or overt threats and intimidation to oppose Christians today. Always remember never to waste your time in engaging the opposition; recognize the underlying person behind each attack - Satan. Never allow yourself to be drawn into the mud, but strategically deal with his schemes through prayer, focus, and the strengthening of your effort to do whatever it takes to forge ahead.

4. DISCOURAGEMENT AND EXHAUSTION

"And Judah said, The strength of the bearers of burdens is decayed, and there is much rubbish; so that we are not able to build the wall. And our adversaries said, They shall not know, neither see, till we come in the midst among them, and slay them, and cause the work to cease" (Nehemiah 4:10-11).

Apparently there was a discouraging proverb or work song that circulated among the workers at this point. They were weary and the piles of rubble they were clearing did not seem to be decreasing. Their stamina was being questioned. There was also the fear of the enemies sneaking into their midst to slay them and cause the work to cease. The workers' earlier zeal for the work - which had resulted in the wall being rapidly built to the halfway mark - was now non-existent (Nehemiah 4:6). Satan knows that the halfway point in any work is the most effective time for him to strike. There is usually a surge of enthusiasm at the onset of any project. However, it is not unlikely for exhaustion and discouragement to set in by the mid-point of the project. The workers in the scripture above felt like quitting.

The same thing is true of us in this present day. We are initially fired up on new projects or endeavors, but if care is not taken, we can become weary. At the onset of our salvation experience, we are enthusiastic and raring to go. You feel like saving the whole world for Christ. You go to every bible study and everything that you hear is fresh and challenging. Your time in the word of God and in prayer are rich with new discoveries.

However, if care is not taken, somewhere down the line, the newness wears off. You begin to notice the piles of rubble in your own life and in the church; problems and sins that just do not seem to go away. You become jaded, wondering if all your efforts are making any difference for the cause of Christ. Your weariness leads to discouragement. This is true for any new adventure you commence. It could be your marriage, a new business venture, new employment, new relationship, etc.

5. INTERNAL NEGATIVISM

The criticism and mockery in Nehemiah 4:2-3 came from the enemy without; but as time progressed, there was internal negativism from the Jews themselves. Those Jews who lived near the enemy (Nehemiah 4:12), were not involved in the work of rebuilding the wall but their closeness to the enemy rubbed off on them and they began to echo the sentiments of the enemy. The worst Satanic attack is that which comes from those closest to you. You must be careful and strategic in dealing with such attacks. As Jesus rightly put it, a house that is divided against itself cannot stand. Internal division is a killer of dreams and visions.

6. FEAR

Fear is the cumulative effect of all the above factors. The people had seen the enemy's anger and had heard their mockery and threats. They were weary from exhaustion. Nehemiah saw their fear and boldly encouraged them not to be afraid. Satan uses fear to paralyze God's people and to keep them from attempting anything significant for the Lord. It may be the fear of failure, fear of the unknown, or fear of rejection. "You have never done it before, and you do not know if you can do it and if you try, others will think you are fanatical and shy away from you." These are some of the thoughts that Satan uses to oppose people's efforts on projects they undertake to advance their destinies.

HOW DO YOU HANDLE OPPOSITION?

Whenever you encounter opposition, you have several options. You can run away from it; try to dodge it; go around it; work out a compromise; or you can meet it head-on and work through it. The last approach is the only biblical way. Nehemiah's approach to handling opposition can be broken down into four aspects.

1. LIFT YOUR VOICE IN PRAYER

Often when we face opposition, our first response is to get angry and hit back or defend ourselves. However, our first response should always be to pray about it. At each point of attack, Nehemiah rallied his people to pray (Nehemiah 4:4, 9). Philippians 4:6 tells us to pray in all things. Prayer gives room for divine intervention. Prayer is an invitation to God for him to step into your situations. Prayer is turning the battle over to God so he can fight the enemy on your behalf. Prayer also gives you strength to face the opposition and launch ahead to build. In 1 Samuel 30, David and 600 men working with him went to war. But on returning, the entire town was burnt down and invaders took their wives and children. David and his men wept bitterly until they had no more strength to weep (1 Samuel 30:4). In verse 8, David called the priest to inquire of God on what to do; which is itself, a form of prayer. John Bunyan wisely observed, "You can do more than pray after you have prayed, but you cannot do more than pray until you have prayed."

2. PUT YOUR HEART INTO THE WORK.

The people had a heart to work (Nehemiah 4:6). They did not allow the enemy's threat to shift their focus onto other issues. Although there was a slight pause when Nehemiah organized his men for work, they did not abandon the work to chase down the enemy. They just kept on building the wall, and soon the enemy was outside looking up, instead of looking straight across at them over the wall. When the Philistines came against Isaac and blocked the well he dug, Isaac opened another well. He kept on digging every time they closed the well. He refused to allow their opposition to stop his effort. Never allow yourself to be distracted by the actions of opposition. Never be distracted by allowing yourself to be drawn into arguments. The intent of every opposition is to distract you, take you off-track, and destroy your attempts to build. Respond with prayer, be tenacious in your work, and refuse to be distracted.

3. KEEP YOUR EYES ON THE ENEMY, IN VIGILANCE

Nehemiah prayed first, but then he set up a guard. Trust God and also be vigilant in mapping out physical plans to overcome the enemy. You must pray as if your protection depends only on prayer, and you must also be vigilant. That you engage in prayer does not mean that you can ignore the enemy's threats or pretend that they do not exist. Nehemiah was vigilant enough to arm the workers and post guards around the clock. He also put in place a warning system, so that wherever the trumpet was blown, the workers would quickly rally there to defend their families and the city. The workers did not take off their clothes at night so that they would be ready to defend the city. What an all rounded vigilant approach! Jesus said in Matthew 26:41, *"Keep watch and pray, so that you will not give in to temptation. For the spirit is willing, but the body is weak!"*

If a report came during a church service that a dangerous lion had escaped in the neighborhood, would you stroll out to your car in normal fashion? Would you let your little child run loose outside? Of course not. You would most likely call 911 for police assistance and also be cautious and watchful. You may even arm yourself and be on guard constantly, for fear of that lion on the loose. As Christians, we must be cautious not to fall prey to the adversary; the devil, who prowls about like a roaring lion, seeking whom to devour. Truly, we need to put on the full armor of God (Ephesians 6:10-20).

Many Christians are oblivious to the dangers that come from the adversary. And to be oblivious to the enemy is to be vulnerable. Some allow themselves to be conformed to worldly views and worldly values. They allow their minds to be filled with the poisonous junk from the worldly systems around us. We allow our minds to be filled with secular humanistic philosophies from TV, social media, etc. If you do not want to fall victim to the enemy, you have to set up a defense mechanism against him, in advance. Block the opportunities for moral filth from your life and home. Spend time each day saturating your mind with God's word. Have a network of close associates whom you can rally together, when the enemy attacks. Nehemiah and his people responded to the enemy's opposition by lifting their voices in prayer, putting their hearts into the work, and carefully keeping their eyes on the enemy.

4. KEEP YOUR MIND FOCUSED ON THE LORD, IN FAITH

Nehemiah reminded the people in Nehemiah 4:14, *"Remember the Lord who is great and awesome and fight for your brothers, your sons, your daughters, your wives and your houses."* The people were discouraged because they focused on the enemy's threats, the pile of rubble, and all the work yet undone. Nehemiah rightly directed their focus back to the Lord who is great and awesome, and to the things that were at stake if they yielded to the enemy. He pointed to the fact that the welfare of their families was at stake, if they take their focus off God.

When opposition hits, it is easy to shift your focus off the Lord and onto your problems. At such times, you need to set your mind on the things from above. Find and understand God's perspective on your situation (Colossians 3:2). You must understand that no matter the trial or the problem, it is not unique to you. It has happened to people before and God delivered them. Keep your mind focused on God, his faithfulness and his ability (1 Corinthians 10:13). If handled properly, opposition can make you stronger, instead of destroying you.

A well-known historian, Will Durant, noted in one of his writings that opposition kept Rome strong. According to him, "The Roman empire remained great as long as she had enemies who forced her to unity, vision, and heroism. When she had overcome all her enemies, she flourished for a moment and then began to die." Just know that if you want to accomplish anything meaningful in life, you will experience opposition, especially if you are in leadership. Respond as Nehemiah did, with prayer, keeping on with work, vigilance against the enemy, and keeping your focus on the great and awesome God whom we serve.

Finally, we need to rise up like Nehemiah and build spiritual walls for our lives, marriages and families. When our spiritual walls are built and continuously fortified with God's words and promises, we will be able to protect vulnerable children from the devices of the devil that seek to capture their minds. We will also be victorious in our faith, family, finances, etc., bringing all glory to God.

NEHEMIAH's STRATEGIES FOR SECURING GOD'S HANDS

To successfully receive and enjoy the favor and the hands of God in his task of rebuilding the wall in 52 days, Nehemiah:

1. Recognized the need of his people, and had a burden to bring about a resolution.
2. Fasted and prayed about the plight of his people.
3. Prayed to God to grant him favor when the King inquired about his sad countenance.
4. Sought favor from the King to undertake his mission to rebuild the wall.
5. Secured all the resources needed to rebuild the walls from the king. Whenever you have a God given vision, you can rest assured, that God will bring likeminded people to support you in accomplishing the goals of the vision.
6. Assessed the volume of the work and outlined his plans, before mobilizing the leaders and nobles to join him on the job.
7. Exhibited intense focus and passion for the project, that it sparked a momentum for all the leaders to join in the work of restoring the fallen walls.
8. Refused to be intimidated by his enemies (Sanballat and Tobiah) to halt the building project.

LESSONS LEARNED FROM NEHEMIAH'S EFFORTS

1. We need to prioritize fasting and prayer towards any great need in our home, church, business, and nation, to secure God's favor and hands upon them, before the enemy comes calling.
2. We need to see our blind spots in our stewardship of our marriage and parenting, our temperament and relationships with others, our communion with God, our time for

Bible studies, our fellowship with the church, developing and using our talents and gifts, planning and managing our businesses, etc. Failure to pray for ourselves, families, churches, and our nation is a great blind spot. Nehemiah did not complain about the sins or weaknesses of Israel's past and present leaders; but rather, he wept, prayed, and fasted, confessing his sins and that of his forefathers that had brought the nation to her deplorable state. Nehemiah found favor with God and with the king because of this, allowing him to rebuild the fallen walls of Jerusalem in a record time of 52 days.

3. Effective and successful work needs collaboration with God and others.

4. We need vision, passion, and planning abilities, together with the necessary grit to motivate people to join us to accomplish any great task.

5. We must stay focused on our work, irrespective of opposition, challenges, and frustrations from the enemy's camp.

4

THE ROLE OF VISION IN YOUR REBUILDING EFFORTS

"And the Lord said unto Abram, after that Lot was separated from him, Lift up now thine eyes, and look from the place where thou art northward, and southward, and eastward, and westward: For all the land which thou seest, to thee will I give it, and to thy seed for ever" (Genesis 13:14-15).

One of the fundamental elements of building or rebuilding a destiny, organization, systems, or any venture at all is vision. Vision is the ability to encapsulate the future at the present time. It is seeing the ultimate, beyond the immediate.

In order for Abraham to be the father of a new nation, he had to envision it. God made sure that he had the vision for it even when there was nothing in his life that reflected it.

"For all the land which thou seest, to thee will I give it, and to thy seed forever" (Genesis 13:15).

God was not just referring to the land Abraham could see with his physical sight, but also his ability to envision. To envision is to dream with your eyes wide open; it is a mental image of what the future will or could entail. Having foresight is the ability to think about or plan the future with imagination and wisdom. Thus, how far ahead you see, determines your accomplishments in life.

When asked how she was successful despite being blind, Helen Keller, the blind author and entrepreneur responded, saying, "Even though I am blind in my eyes, I am not blind in my mind." She considered blind minds worse than blind eyes, equating blind minds to having sight, but no vision. Franklin Roosevelt, a former American President who suffered from polio and used a wheelchair, also considered a lack of vision as a disability that is much more incapacitating than a lack of mobility. How you think does determine how you live (Proverbs 23:7). You cannot think small and live large. Neither can you think large and live small. It is impossible to think like a grasshopper and live like an eagle (Numbers 13:33).

THINGS TO KNOW ABOUT VISION

Vision contradicts your present reality. Since vision is futuristic, it will contradict your present. When the Israelites were slaves in Egypt, God gave them a vision of a land flowing with milk and honey. A true vision will show you an image of a place better than where you are currently. If you look into the next ten years and see your today, then you do not have a vision.

Vision will confront your sense of comfort. It shakes you from your sense of ease. It will make a timid person bold or a happy-go-lucky person, daring. A true vision will make you uncomfortable and challenge your current norms. It will challenge your laziness. All of us want to live a comfortable life, but there is a level of comfort that is not comfortable. That unwanted level is one of complacency where the belief is that God will do it with no input from you. However, there are things God does and there are things we must do (Joshua 13:1).

HOW DOES VISION ENHANCE YOUR ABILITY TO BUILD OR REBUILD?

1. The vision you have in your heart determines the opportunities, people, resources, etc., that will be attracted to you.
2. The size of vision determines the size of your plan, and the size of your plan determines the size of your action. Those who see big, plan big, act big and experience bigger outcomes.
3. Vision is the fuel for speed (Habakkuk 2:2).
4. What a man sees determines what God gives (Genesis 13:14). If you have a great vision, God will give you even greater outcomes.
5. Vision is a necessary aspect of faith, and faith is key to any meaningful endeavor.

The extent to which a vision impacts future outcomes is exemplified by the Shunamite widow in 2 Kings 4:1-7. She had a small jar of oil and was instructed by the prophet to borrow vessels from her neighbors, close the door, and pour the oil in the vessels.

As soon as her vessels were used up, the oil ceased to flow.

> *"When the vessels were all full, she said to her son, Bring me another vessel. And he said to her, There is not a one left. Then the oil stopped multiplying" [2 Kings 4:6 (Amp.)].*

The oil stopped multiplying when she no longer had the vision to capture it in the jars. The problem was not shortage of oil (provision) but of the vessels (vision). Where vision stops; there provision stops. It is the limit of imagination and foresight that limits God, and never the shortage of supplies (Ephesians 3:20). What you imagine is what will emerge. Wherever there is a God-ordained vision, there will always be provision.

COMPONENTS OF A VISION

A true godly vision has three components.

1. **Foresight**, which is like looking through a telescope. Just like a telescope, foresight helps you to bring things that are far away, nearer. Foresight allows you to look through the telescope of life to see the next 1-, 2-, 3- and more years ahead. The good thing is that everyone has the capacity to operate in this manner. A person who wants to achieve much in life should be able to look into the telescope of life and plan his/her years ahead.
2. **Insight**. Under a microscope, you are able to see things in more detailed form. Insight gives you an understanding

of what to do from here and now, so you can reach your desired destination revealed to you by foresight. Joseph had a foresight about the famine in Egypt and also gave the king an insight on solving the famine problem.

"Let Pharaoh do this, and let him appoint officers over the land, to collect one-fifth of the produce of the land of Egypt in the seven plentiful years. And let them gather all the food of those good years that are coming, and store up grain under the authority of Pharaoh, and let them keep food in the cities. Then that food shall be as a reserve for the land for the seven years of famine which shall be in the land of Egypt, that the land may not perish during the famine" [Genesis 41:34-36 (NKJV)]

In the natural, the microscope helps you to see the details; similarly, insight gives you an understanding of the smaller details required to accomplish your plans.

3. **A Workable Plan.** Every nation that moved from being third world to first world had a clear plan and worked towards it. Every company that grew from a living room-type to a multi-level facility had a detailed vision for it from the onset, and worked towards the set goal. And every human being that became a success had a vision, backed up with a workable plan. In life things do not just happen, and must be carefully orchestrated to succeed.

HOW DO YOU CAPTURE A VISION?

The bible provides us with many examples of useful strategies for capturing a vision.

1. Prayerfully stay in the word of God and see your future from the pages of the word. Use scriptures to paint a better picture of your future. In fact, another definition of a vision is your future as captured from the scripture. Every scripture is an actual prophecy of your future

    "I will stand upon my watch, and set me upon the tower, and will watch to see what he will say unto me, and what I shall answer when I am reproved" (Habakkuk 2:1).

    As you prayerfully meditate in the word of God, the Holy Spirit will quicken your spirit or your mind and release images, pictures or plans of your future into your heart.

2. Through spiritual revelation. An example was Apostle Paul who received a vision through a spiritual revelation in Acts 26:12-19. It can either be through a dream or a prophetic word (Habakkuk 2:2).

3. Through deep concern for situations around you. That was the case with Nehemiah. He received the vision to rebuild the wall of Jerusalem from a deep concern for the circumstances of the land (Nehemiah 1:1-4). His vision did not come as a result of supernatural revelation like Paul. It came because he received information about the condition of Jerusalem and his people, and he became concerned.

God sometimes allows you to see a problem because you already have the solution. It must always, however, be linked to God's plan for your life, because you are not here to solve every problem you see. It is always important to hear from God concerning the problem to make sure it is in line with God's plan for your life. That way, it will not be what can be called a "me, too" vision; one where somebody has it, and so you must as well. Your vision must be related to your destiny.

4. Through the culture of healthy imitation (John 15:4-5). Even with a vision similar to someone else's, you cannot do anything unless your vision is linked to God.

5. Through association and impartation. A vision can be received through association and impartation. Joshua was a biblical example.

"Now Joshua the son of Nun was full of the spirit of wisdom, for Moses had laid his hands on him; so the children of Israel heeded him, and did as the LORD had commanded Moses" [Deuteronomy 34:9 (NKJV)].

How did Joshua receive his vision? By being around a man of vision, he caught a vision and received an impartation. Joshua's vision was the same as Moses' vision. He was raised alongside Moses and he understood the vision of Moses. He stayed so close to Moses that God gave Joshua the same commission he gave to Moses.

All of these are valid ways through which you can catch a vision. As such, that you have not received a revelation, been in a trance, or heard a supernatural voice from heaven, does not mean you cannot be a visionary.

WHAT TO DO WITH YOUR VISION

1. Embrace it; make plans, and pursue the vision for its manifestation.

2. Act promptly (Habakkuk 2:2). A large vision requires significant actions.

3. You do not sleep on the vision; but you run with it. Vision not pursued is vision that will perish no matter how real it is. The mandate has to be pursued, for it to be delivered, since every vision has a time frame; it is yet for an appointed time. You do not have eternity to fulfill your vision. If you sleep on it, it may elude you.

4. Depend on God for the strength and provision for fulfilling the vision. Vision cannot be accomplished with the energy of your flesh, but in the power of the spirit. Only the hand of God can deliver the plan of God. What his mouth has spoken, his hand has also performed (1 Kings 8:56).

5. The prayer of faith gives you access to the hand of God. It takes faith to deliver any divine mandate.

One of the keys responsible for the success of Nehemiah was prayer (Nehemiah 1:4).

Prayer was one of the engines that drove the destiny of Jesus Christ (Luke 3:21).

"And it came to pass in those days, that he went out into a mountain to pray, and continued all night in prayer to God. And when it was day, he called unto him his disciples: and of them he chose twelve, whom also he named apostles; Simon, (whom he also named Peter,) and Andrew his brother, James and John, Philip and Bartholomew," (Luke 6:12-13).
"And when he had sent them away, he departed into a mountain to pray. And when even was come, the ship in the midst of the sea (Luke 9:28; Mark 6:46).

a. Prayer gives birth to vision. The ALCC vision was birthed in prayer. And when prayers give birth to vision, watchfulness keeps the vision in remembrance. Watchfulness allows alertness and gives direction to vision.

   "I will stand upon my watch and set me upon the towers and will watch to see what he will say unto me" (Habakkuk 2:2).

b. Prayer helps to overcome opposition to your vision. Many visions have been snatched through prayerlessness (Nehemiah 4:4, 9). Nehemiah prayed all along to overcome obstacles to his vision. Prayer makes your battles and struggles, God's battle. Prayer moves you beyond people and any spirit.

c. Prayer attracts resources to your vision (Nehemiah 2:4-8; James 4:1)

d. Prayer gives you the strength to pursue your vision.

"For the vision is yet for an appointed time, but at the end it shall speak, and not lie: though it tarry, wait for it; because it will surely come, it will not tarry" (Habakkuk 2:3).

Discouragement may set in, but prayer is the fuel that fires your engine (Isaiah 40:29-30).

5

THE ROLE OF PASSION IN YOUR REBUILDING EFFORT.

Passion is what motivates you to pursue your dreams, despite opposition, danger and challenges. It is what makes you to persevere in the face of criticisms and discouragement. Mount Everest in Nepal is the world's highest mountain standing at the height of 29,029 ft. About 800 people try to climb it annually. Over 375 people have died trying to climb it. Despite the difficulty in climbing the mountain and the risk of death, passion is the reason why many still try to climb it.

Nothing great is ever accomplished or sustained in life without passion.

> *"And let us not grow weary of doing good, for in due season we will reap, if we do not give up" (Galatians 6:9).*

Where your passion stops is where your pursuit stops; and that is also where your harvest stops.

Passion is what energizes life. It is what makes the impossible possible. Passion is what gives you the reason to get up in the morning and go. Without passion, life becomes a routine, boring, monotonous, and dull. Your passion keeps you going when everyone else has quit. It keeps you working hard when everyone else has stopped.

From the simplest to the most sophisticated goal in life, passion is needed in order to succeed. You cannot fulfill destiny or become successful if you are not passionate about life or about what you are doing. One of the ways the enemy can stop your progress is to reduce your passion for the pursuit of your goals.

WHAT IS PASSION?

Passion, from the dictionary, is a strong feeling of enthusiasm or excitement for doing something. Passion is what motivates you to become the very best you can be. The Holy Ghost through Apostle Paul gave us the perspective to life and the pursuit of purpose in Philippians 3:13-14 (TLB).

> *"No, dear brothers, I am still not all I should be, but I am bringing all my energies to bear on this one thing: Forgetting the past and looking forward to what lies ahead, [14] I strain to reach the end of the race and receive the prize for which God is calling us up to heaven because of what Christ Jesus did for us" [Philippians 3:13-14 (TLB)].*

Apostle Paul was passionate about attaining the goal set for him by God, and he was ready to press on despite the threat of imprisonment and ultimate threat of death. Passion is the fuel for the pursuit of your dream. While strength speaks of supernatural empowerment given by the Holy Spirit, passion speaks of emotional strength. You may have spiritual empowerment but if passion is lacking, you may still fail to perform. That was the case with prophet Elijah.

"And Ahab told Jezebel all that Elijah had done, also how he had executed all the prophets with the sword. 2 Then Jezebel sent a messenger to Elijah, saying, "So let the gods do to me, and more also, if I do not make your life as the life of one of them by tomorrow about this time." 3 And when he saw that, he arose and ran for his life, and went to Beersheba, which belongs to Judah, and left his servant there. 4 But he himself went a day's journey into the wilderness, and came and sat down under a [a]broom tree. And he prayed that he might die, and said, "It is enough! Now, Lord, take my life, for I am no better than my fathers!"(1 Kings 19:1-4).

From the above scripture, Elijah lost the passion to forge ahead in his earthly assignment because of the threat from Jezebel, and because of the erroneous belief of being the only one still standing in the service of God in the midst of hostility. As a result of the loss of the passion to pursue his assignment, God instructed him to prepare others to take his place, and took him to heaven.

It is practically impossible to pursue or rebuild your vision in the absence of passion. Passion is required, to be willing to endure whatever is necessary for the cause with which you identify. The most famous example is the passion of Jesus Christ. It was not fun to go through what Jesus went through on the cross, but he persevered.

> *"Father, if you are willing, take this cup from me; yet not my will, but yours be done"* (Luke 22:42).

As great as it is, passion can be difficult to maintain at times. After months or perhaps years of doing the same thing, our fervor and enthusiasm can wane. When you lose your passion, suddenly things stop making sense like they used too. Things you once loved doing cease to matter. Therefore, we must be mindful of things that can reduce, or kill our passion.

FACTORS THAT AFFECTS PASSION (PASSION KILLERS)

Living without purpose. Passion dissipates when you lack purpose. Living without purpose is the most common reason people lack passion. As Rick Warren said, you can be driven by guilt, resentment, anger, fear, materialism, or the need for approval. All will lead to the same end – an unfulfilled life and unnecessary stress. It is usually meaningless work and not overwork that wears people down, saps their strength and robs them of joy. Without God, life has no purpose. Without purpose, life has no meaning. Without meaning, life has no significance or hope. Without a clear purpose, you will keep changing direction, jobs, relationships, churches and other things; hoping each change will settle your confusion or fill the emptiness of life.

When Jesus stood before Pontius Pilate to be sentenced to death, Pilate made a statement of purpose in John 18:37.

> *"Pilate therefore said unto him, Art thou a king then? Jesus answered, Thou sayest that I am a king. To this end was I born, and for this cause came I into the world, that I should bear witness unto the truth. Every one that is of the truth heareth my voice" (John 18:37).*

Jesus had the opportunity to take the path of least resistance, avoid dying, and ultimately fail in fulfilling his purpose. The revelation of his purpose helped him to willingly embrace his death on the cross. The more your purpose centers on God and his plan for your life and eternity, the more passionate you are going to be about living, and the more fully alive you are going to be. If your purpose is just to make money, you will have no reason to live after making the money. If your purpose is just to get married, you will have no reason to live after the marriage.

Negative places. The places we go affect the passion within us. Your life changes by the knowledge you gain and the people you meet. The places you go determine the people you see, and the people you see determine the favor you enjoy. The favor you experience, determines the result you have. Our dreams can be compared to seeds. Seeds do not just grow in any soil. The quality of the soil is critical to the growth of the seed, because the nutrient the seed will need to grow is in the soil. Favor goes a long way to determine how far you go (Psalms 30:7). In order to sustain your passion, you need to intentionally position yourself in an atmosphere conducive for igniting your passion (Proverbs 4:14-19).

Exposure to wrong or toxic words. Nothing kills passion like exposure to toxic or wrong words. Words are very powerful. While we must be open to correction, we cannot survive when we are constantly exposed to destiny-killing words. Words are either life-giving or life-taking; encouraging or discouraging; uplifting or demoralizing.

> *"Death and life are in the power of the tongue, And those who love it will eat its fruit" [Proverbs 18:21 (NKJV)].*

HOW TO RENEW YOUR PASSION

Remember your purpose. By remembering why you started, you can rekindle your enthusiasm and renew your passion. When David was confronted by the jealous attacks by one of his brothers, Eliab, at the battle front, his understanding of the reason for the battle prevailed. He knew what was at stake against the nation and the name of his God. He replied his brother, saying, "Is there not a cause?"

> *"And Eliab his eldest brother heard when he spake unto the men; and Eliab's anger was kindled against David, and he said, Why camest thou down hither? and with whom hast thou left those few sheep in the wilderness? I know thy pride, and the naughtiness of thine heart; for thou art come down that thou*

mightest see the battle. And David said, What have I now done? Is there not a cause?" (1 Samuel 17:28-29).

In Hebrews 12:1-2, Jesus endured the shame and pain on the cross because of the cause. The joy ahead, was the liberation and total salvation of mankind. Elisha persevered to the end in 2 Kings 2:1-6, despite all obstacles, because he set his mind of the purpose. Why did you start that venture? Why are you in that marital relationship? Why are you pursuing that goal? What is your desired end that made you commence the journey? Have you lost your focus on the reason?

Associate with passionate people. They are called firelighters and passion boosters. They are those who walk into your life and your passion goes up. They are those that even if you are feeling down before meeting them, your passion is ignited in their presence. Yet, there are those who walk into your life and your passion nosedives.

"Iron sharpeneth iron; so a man sharpeneth the countenance of his friend" (Proverbs 27:17)

Having passionate people in your life, dramatically increases your own passion levels. Hence, when you feel as though you need to renew your passion for a purpose, give that passionate person you know a call, so they can encourage and get you up again.

Learn something new. According to professionals, learning new skills helps greatly in overcoming boredom. Learning new things keeps your interest level high so you do not get bored as easily.

Learning breaks the cycle of monotony and prevents boredom from setting in. You also become a more interesting person. Well-rounded individuals have an easier time relating to others and have more things in common with them. Being a more interesting person will draw others to you and improve the quality of your life as your relationships improve and deepen.

Learning something new lights up our brains and engages our senses, and can powerfully reignite our passion at work. Your brain chemistry changes. The white matter in your brain is called myelin, and it helps improve performance on a number of tasks. The more people practice a new skill they are learning, the more dense the myelin in their brains becomes, which helps them learn even better. When was the last time you learned something new? Increase your knowledge of your field by taking new study courses.

The wonderful thing is that it does not have to be something big. It can be something small that takes less than five minutes to learn. For example, you could learn how to color code email messages by sender, so you can more effectively prioritize incoming messages. Or, how to use keyboard shortcuts to auto-populate text in email messages. Learn one new thing and watch your excitement return.

Introduce creativity. Introduce creativity into what you do, by doing the same routine, differently. The same routine day after day can become monotonous, dull and mind numbing. We can be managing calendars, tasks, and work responsibilities in a manner that no longer challenge or excite us. We may be following patterns or routines that may no longer align with our current goals and objectives, nor the strategic priorities of the organization. Continuous passion demands that we break out of the status quo. Be ready and willing to employ a different approach while you still obtain the same result.

RECHARGE! REFRESH! RENEW!

No matter how powerful your phone device is, when the battery runs down, it becomes useless. We are created to need rest. Even God rested. At creation, God worked for six and rested on the seventh day. Having finished, God blessed the seventh day and declared it holy. God thinks rest from work is so important that he set one day apart from his work to rest. It has been scientifically proven that lack of rest significantly affects the quality of our health. Health goes down and we literarily can lose many years. Our performance level also goes down, and our stress level goes up (Luke 8:22-24).

The sabbath is not a religion of not worshipping on a certain day, but a principle of rest and refreshing. Jesus Christ who became man showed us how to live victoriously on the earth.

> *"At evening, when the sun had set, they brought to Him all who were sick and those who were demon-possessed. And the whole city was gathered together at the door. Then He healed many who were sick with various diseases, and cast out many demons; and He did not allow the demons to speak, because they knew Him. Now in the morning, having risen a long while*

before daylight, He went out and departed to a solitary place;
and there He prayed. And Simon and those who were with Him
searched for Him (Mark 1:32-36).
"But Jesus often withdrew to lonely places and prayed" (Luke
5:16).

In our always-on, hyper-connected, 24/7 busy culture, our work can quickly consume us and our time. In an effort to catch up, keep up, or get ahead, we work every day of the week. To fully recharge and be ready to engage at work, learn to recharge. Just let your mind and body rest.

A break or time away provides:

- Fresh perspectives
- Time for your body and mind to get some much-needed rest
- An opportunity for new ideas to develop
- The space you need to evaluate things properly and make thought out decisions.
- Rest, and watch your passion come back to life.

THE GREATEST PRAYER
OF ALL TIME

The greatest prayer of a lifetime is to be reconnected back to God in a living relationship. Relationship is the basis for asking. You cannot pray to a God who you do not know and who does not know you. God wants to be intimate with you. This type of relationship is available to each one of us when we sincerely repent of our sins, ask for God's forgiveness, and receive His Son, Jesus, as our personal Lord and Savior. If you have never surrendered your life to God, or if you have turned away from God and you want to return to Him, now is the time. God is waiting for you. His arms are open wide to receive you. Just pray this simple prayer right now:

"O Lord, be merciful to me, a sinner. I realize that I am a sinner. I need a savior and you are my savior. I repent of every sin, every wrongdoing, and I ask for your forgiveness. I receive Jesus Christ, Your only begotten Son, as my Lord and my Savior. I believe that Jesus went to the cross for me and paid the price for my salvation, and now I receive Him into my heart. I declare that I am born again. I am a child of God. Old sins are gone, and I have a brand-new life in Christ, in Jesus' Name. Amen."

NOTES

NOTES

NOTES

NOTES

www.ingramcontent.com/pod-product-compliance
Lightning Source LLC
Chambersburg PA
CBHW071423040426
42445CB00012BA/1269